My Name Is Nura

written by Anne M. Castagliola
illustrated by Donna Perrone

Macmillan
McGraw-Hill

New York   Farmington

My name is Nura and I am eight years old. We say my name like this: NOOR-UH. My family lives in the Arabian Desert.

Most people in the Middle East live in houses. But I am a Bedouin (BED-OU-WIN). My people live in the desert. We never stay in one place for too long.

Our home is a beautiful tent, which is made of hair from our camels. Inside we use colorful rugs and blankets instead of furniture. This makes it easier when we have to move. It would be hard to move tables and chairs on the back of a camel!

We don't have kitchens. Instead, we cook our food over a fire.

It's the children's job to get wood for the fire every day. We also help to take down and put up the tents when we have to move.

Our tents are very important to us. They keep the hot sun away and keep the sand away from us when it's windy.

We raise camels and that is why we have to move so often. In the spring, we look to see where the rain has fallen and we go there. We cannot stay a long time in the same place because our camels eat up all the grass. We go where the water is. Places in the desert that have water and grass and sometimes trees are called oases.

My brothers and sisters and friends and I have fun in many ways. We run with our dogs and play games together. We laugh and cheer for each other.

Sometimes after the evening meal we sing songs, or our mothers and fathers will tell stories of long ago. We sit by the fire and soon we fall asleep. You may wonder why we have a fire at night. It's hot during the day, but nights in the desert can be cold.

Sometimes we go to towns or villages. We trade camel skins, milk, and meat for grains, dates, and other food. But most of the time we live out in the desert, where it is hot and dry.

In the desert there are no buildings, schools or shops. If there is an accident, there is no police or fire station to call. If my little brother slips and falls, my father or mother comes to wipe his tears. Not many people live out here in the desert. When I sing, my audience is my family and the other people I live with.

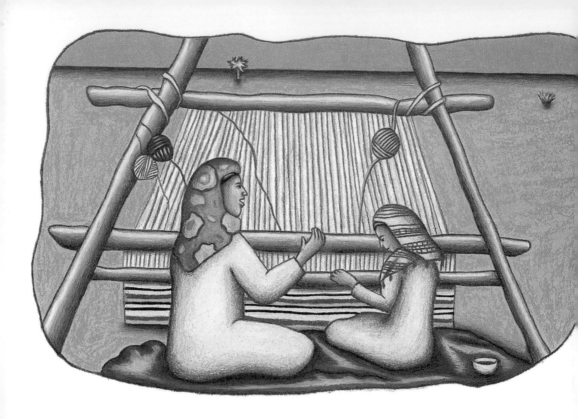

How do we live here, you may wonder, where there is little food, little water, and no stores? One reason we can live here is because we raise camels.

Camels are very important to us because from them we get milk and meat. They are also valuable because we ride them from place to place and use them to carry things. We make tents, clothes, and beautiful blankets with camel's hair. My mother is teaching me how to do this.

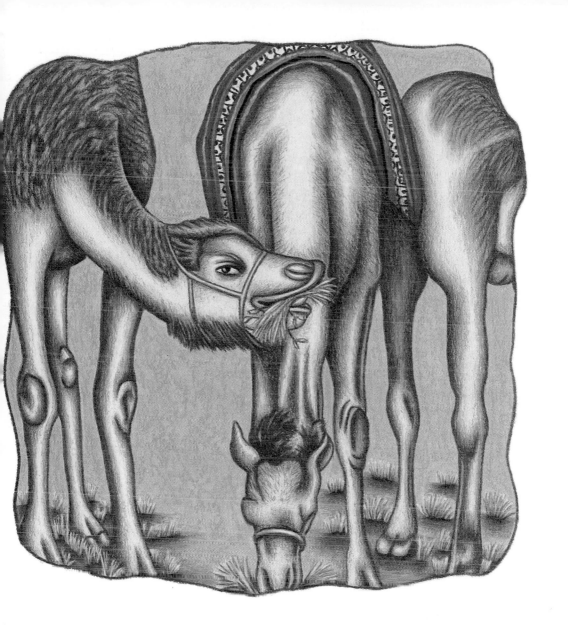

Camels were built for the desert. Grasses, bushes, and dry branches are all great food for a camel. They can get a little water from the plants they eat, and camels will eat almost anything! Their special thick lips protect them from thorns.

When the hot winds blow, camels can close up their noses so that no sand gets in. They can keep sand and sun out of their eyes and ears with their thick lashes and hairy ears. Their feet are extra wide and this keeps them from sinking in the sand.

Most of all, camels are very strong. They can bend down low to the ground. Their knees have special pads to protect them from the burning sand. Our camels carry everything when we have to move. Our tents, our clothes, our pots and pans are all put on the backs of camels.

But camels are not always gentle and
sweet! They know just how much they can
carry. If we put too much on the camel's
back, it won't stand up. It yells and spits at
us! Then if we take some things off, the
camel will stand up and begin its slow, funny
walk through the desert. Camels are very
strong—strong enough to hold a grown man.

Another way camels are built for the desert is that they can live with little food and water.

Because camels are large, it takes longer for the sun to make them hot. Think of how long a big pot of water takes to boil. A smaller pot heats up faster. In the desert, smaller animals get hot sooner than bigger animals.

The kind of camel that we have is called a dromedary. Some kinds of camels have two humps, but ours have only one. Did you think the hump was filled with water? Wrong! The camel's hump is filled with fat. When there is little food, the camel uses this fat for energy.

When a camel's hump is very big, you know that there's a lot of food around. When the hump is little, that camel has not had much to eat in a long time. Camels can drink up to 35 gallons in one day, when they are around water.

Our life in the desert is not easy. We all work together every day to find enough food and water, for ourselves and for our animals. But after a long day, when the moon smiles down over the silent desert sand and the stars shine in the deep blue sky, we sit together around our fire and sing to each other. We listen to the stories of our people from long ago. We know that our life of moving from place to place is good.